W9-BQU-600

THE UNDERTAKER:
REST IN PEACE

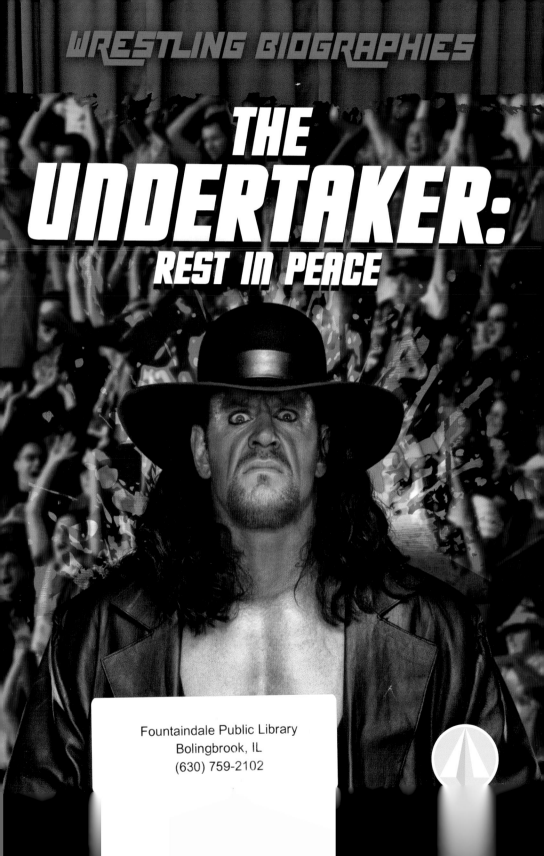

abdobooks.com

Published by Abdo Zoom, a division of ABDO, P.O. Box 398166, Minneapolis, Minnesota 55439. Copyright © 2020 by Abdo Consulting Group, Inc. International copyrights reserved in all countries. No part of this book may be reproduced in any form without written permission from the publisher. Fly!™ is a trademark and logo of Abdo Zoom.

Printed in the United States of America, North Mankato, Minnesota.
052019
092019

Photo Credits: Alamy, AllWrestlingSuperstars.com, Getty Images, Seth Poppel/ Yearbook Library, Shutterstock, © Ed Webster p4 / CC BY 2.0, © Mandy Coombes p11 / CC BY-SA 2.0, © Vishal Somaiya p12 / CC BY-SA 2.0, © Simon Q p13, p14 / CC BY 2.0, © Miguel Discart p15, p20 / CC BY-SA 2.0
Production Contributors: Kenny Abdo, Jennie Forsberg, Grace Hansen
Design Contributors: Dorothy Toth, Neil Klinepier

Library of Congress Control Number: 2018963798

Publisher's Cataloging-in-Publication Data

Names: Abdo, Kenny, author.
Title: The Undertaker: rest in peace / by Kenny Abdo.
Other title: Rest in peace
Description: Minneapolis, Minnesota : Abdo Zoom, 2020 | Series: Wrestling
    biographies set 2 | Includes online resources and index.
Identifiers: ISBN 9781532127564 (lib. bdg.) | ISBN 9781532128547 (ebook) |
    ISBN 9781532129032 (Read-to-me ebook)
Subjects: LCSH: Undertaker, 1965- (Mark Calloway)--Juvenile literature. |
    Wrestlers--United States--Biography--Juvenile literature. | World Wrestling
    Entertainment Studios--Juvenile literature.
Classification: DDC 796.812092 [B]--dc23

TABLE OF CONTENTS

The Undertaker 4

Early Years 6

WWE 10

Legacy 18

Glossary 22

Online Resources 23

Index 24

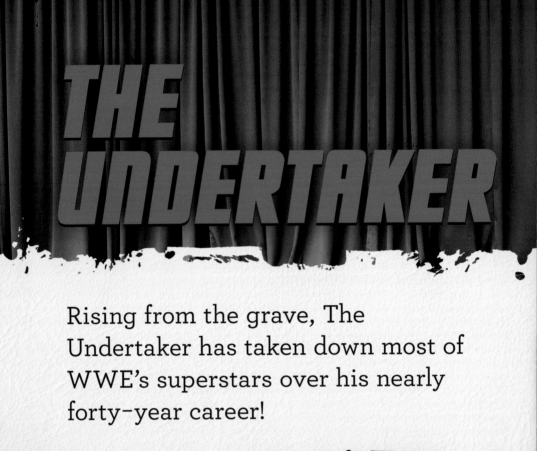

THE UNDERTAKER

Rising from the grave, The Undertaker has taken down most of WWE's superstars over his nearly forty-year career!

He has gone by many names. But The Undertaker will be remembered as one of the greatest wrestlers in WWE history.

EARLY YEARS

Mark Calaway was born in Houston, Texas, in 1965.

At nearly seven feet tall, Calaway has always been athletic. He played many sports in high school. In college, he was a star basketball player for Texas Wesleyan University.

Calaway left college early for professional wrestling. In 1984 he **debuted** in the World Class Championship Wrestling (WCCW). He went by the name Texas Red. In 1989, he fought as The Master of Pain. He won his first **championship** against wrestling icon Jerry Lawler.

The Undertaker made his WWE **debut** during the 1990 **Survivor Series**. He **submitted** Koko B. Ware within a minute of the **match** starting.

The Undertaker has been part of many WWE firsts. He fought in the first **Casket Match** in 1992. He fought in the first **Buried Alive match** in 1996. The Undertaker also entered the first-ever **Hell in a Cell** match.

He brawled in WrestleMania 7 in 1991 and easily defeated Superfly Jimmy Snuka. The Undertaker had a WrestleMania winning streak for more than two decades!

Brock Lesner ended The
Undertaker's winning streak
at WrestleMania 30. He took a
second loss from Roman Reigns at
WrestleMania 33. The Undertaker
returned the next year to beat John
Cena in a single **match**!

LEGACY

The Undertaker was added to the *Guinness Book of World Records* in 2015. It was for his incredible 21-0 WrestleMania winning streak!

The Undertaker is also a big animal lover. He created the Zeus Compton Calaway Save the Animals fund after his dog died. It helped raise money for lifesaving treatments for animals, specifically dogs.

GLOSSARY

Buried Alive – an event where a wrestler throws their opponent into a six-foot deep grave to win.

Casket Match – a wrestling event where a wrestler wins by completely concealing their opponent in a casket.

championship – a game, match, or race held to find a first-place winner.

debut – to appear for the first time.

Hell in a Cell – an event where wrestlers fight in a 20-foot-tall cell. The only way to win is a submission or pinball inside of the cell.

match – a competition in which wrestlers fight against each other.

submit – when a wrestler is able to make their opponent give up.

Survivor Series – a major WWE show held every year in November.

ONLINE RESOURCES

Booklinks
NONFICTION NETWORK
FREE! ONLINE NONFICTION RESOURCES

To learn more about
The Undertaker, please visit
abdobooklinks.com or scan
this QR code. These links
are routinely monitored and
updated to provide the most
current information available.

INDEX

Buried Alive 12

Casket Match 12

Cena, John 16

Guinness Book of World Records 18

Hell in a Cell 12

Lawler, Jerry 9

Lesner, Brock 16

Reigns, Roman 16

Snuka, "Superfly" Jimmy 15

Texas 6

Ware, Koko B. 10

World Class Championship Wrestling (WCCW) 9

WrestleMania 15, 16, 18

WWE 4, 5, 10

Zeus Compton Calaway Save the Animals fund 20